THIS WALKER BOOK BELONGS TO:

_____

_____

_____

_____

First published 1994
by Walker Books Ltd, 87 Vauxhall Walk
London SE11 5HJ

This edition published 1996

10 9 8 7 6 5 4 3

Text © 1994 Foxbusters Ltd
Illustrations © 1994 Anita Jeram

This book has been typeset in Baskerville.

Printed in Hong Kong

British Library Cataloguing in Publication Data
A catalogue record for this book
is available from the British Library.

ISBN 0-7445-4725-3

I LOVE
GUINEA-PIGS

Written by

Dick King-Smith

Illustrated by

Anita Jeram

WALKER BOOKS
AND SUBSIDIARIES
LONDON • BOSTON • SYDNEY

There's a silly old saying that
if you hold a guinea-pig up
by its tail, its eyes
will drop out.

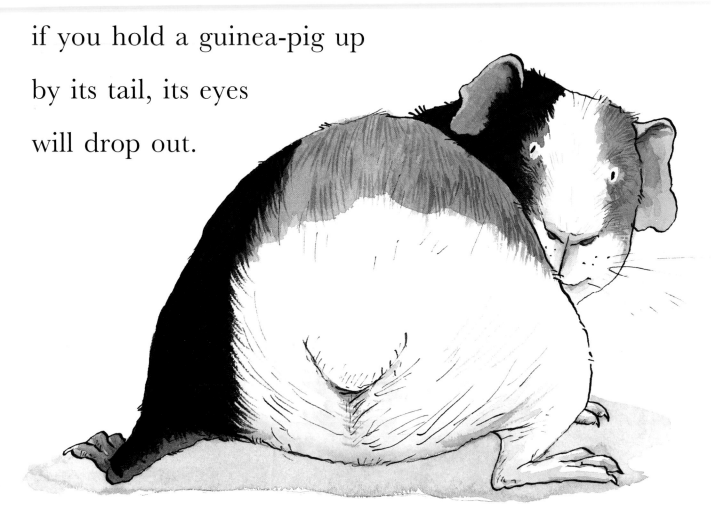

Well of course they wouldn't,
even if you could. Which you couldn't,
because guinea-pigs don't have tails.

What do guinea-pigs
have in common with pigs?

The males and females are
known as "boars" and "sows".

And they aren't pigs either.

They're rodents – like mice and rats
and squirrels.

Rodents have special front teeth
which are brilliant for gnawing things.
These teeth go on growing throughout
the animal's life, and are self-sharpening.

7

As for the other bit of their name, guinea-pigs were first brought to Europe about four hundred years ago by Spanish sailors, probably from a country in South America called Dutch Guiana. And the sailors called them "guiana pigs".

In fact the guinea-pig is a member
of the cavy family, and its
Latin name is *Cavia porcellus*
(which means a piggy-looking cavy).

Anyway, whatever they're called,
it's the way they look that I've
always liked. They're so
chunky and chubby
and cuddly, with their blunt
heads and sturdy bodies and short legs.

Smooth

Peruvian

They come in loads of different colours, and
they can be smooth-coated or rough-coated
or long-coated, not to mention
the other varieties.
I've kept hundreds of
guinea-pigs over the last fifty years,
but I've always liked the Abyssinians best.

Crested

Sheltie

Abyssinians

Guinea-pigs are such sensible animals.

They're awfully easy to keep,

because they aren't fussy.

They don't like the cold, of course, or the damp, any more than you would, and they're not happy living in a poky little place, any more than you would be. But as long as they have a comfortable warm dry place to live, guinea-pigs are as happy as Larry.

Guinea-pigs like a really big roomy hutch, or, better still, a wire run out on the grass.

They're hardy animals, and don't often fall ill. Properly looked after, they can live a long time.

Most guinea-pigs live for around five to eight years.

I once had a Crested sow
called Zen. She lived two years
with me and then eight more
with one of my daughters.
People's hair grows whiter
as they age, but Zen's
grew darker.

Guinea-pigs need plenty of food.

They love eating, just like you do, and feeding them is half the fun of keeping them.

Some people, of course, feed them nothing but hay and pellets from the pet shop and they're quite all right. But how boring a diet like that must be, both for the piggy-looking cavy and its owner.

I always used to give my
guinea-pigs lots of other kinds
of food as well: cabbage and cauliflower leaves,
carrots, bits of bread and apple peelings, and
wild plants like dandelion
and clover. I gave them
 water, too, of course.
Guinea-pigs need
clean drinking
water every day. And their water
bottle often needs washing,
because they like blowing bits
of food back up the spout.

One especially nice thing

about guinea-pigs is that

if you handle them

regularly, and carry them about, stroke

them, talk to them, and make a fuss

of them, they become really

fond of you.

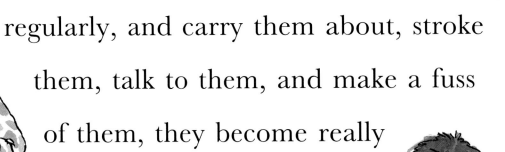

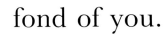

The proper way to pick up
a guinea-pig is with one hand
over its shoulders and the other
supporting its bottom.

19

Another nice thing about guinea-pigs is that they talk a lot.

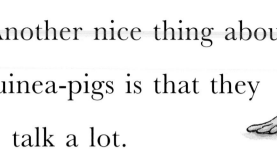

When they want food or water, they often give a sort of whistle, sometimes low, sometimes loud.

Boars say CHUTTER when they're squaring up for a fight.

So do sows when their babies pester them too much.

Other things guinea-pigs say are

PUTT CHUT TWEET and DRR.

But when one guinea-pig says PURR to another

guinea-pig, it's as plain as the nose on your face

that it only means one thing:

"I love you."

And that brings me on
to what's best of all about
keeping guinea-pigs – baby ones.
Because their ancestors, the wild cavies
of South America, lived out in the
open with enemies all about them,
their young ones had to be
ready to run for it.

So the guinea-pig sow carries
her unborn litter for a very
long time, about seventy days,
and they arrive in
the world fully furred, with their
eyes open and their mouths already
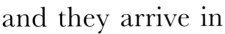
filled with teeth.
Newborn guinea-pigs
are such a comical sight.
Their heads and feet look too big for their bodies.

Baby rabbits are born blind and naked and helpless, but not baby guinea-pigs.

But almost immediately

they show an interest in those two

favourite guinea-pig pursuits –

 eating

and conversation.

Of all the guinea-pigs I've kept, there were two that I shall never forget. Both were Abyssinians, both were boars, and each in his time fathered dozens of lovely big-headed, big-footed babies.

One was a bright golden colour,
and his name was King Arthur.
The other was a blue roan called
Beach Boy. Both are buried in
my garden.

There's a solitary apple tree at the edge
of my lawn, and I like to look at it and think
that under it Beach Boy and King Arthur
lie peacefully, one on one side of the tree,
one on the other.

I'm not sad about this –
just happy to remember
what a lot of pleasure
I've had from all
my guinea-pigs.

INDEX

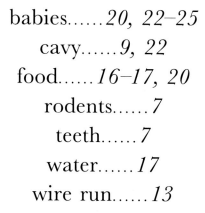

Look up the pages to find out
about all these guinea-pig things.
Don't forget to look at both kinds
of words: this kind and **this kind.**

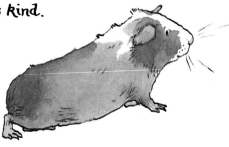

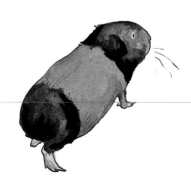

MORE WALKER PAPERBACKS
For You to Enjoy

"These books fulfil all the requirements of a factual picture book, but also supply that imaginative element." *The Independent on Sunday*

"Beautifully illustrated books, written with style and humour."
The Times Educational Supplement

I LOVE GUINEA-PIGS
by Dick King-Smith/Anita Jeram
0-7445-4725-3   £4.99

ALL PIGS ARE BEAUTIFUL
by Dick King-Smith/Anita Jeram
0-7445-3635-9   £4.99

RED FOX
by Karen Wallace/Peter Melnyczuk
0-7445-4361-4   £4.99

TOWN PARROT
by Penelope Bennett/Sue Heap
0-7445-4727-X   £4.99

I LIKE MONKEYS BECAUSE...
by Peter Hansard/Patricia Casey
0-7445-3646-4   £4.99

THINK OF AN EEL
by Karen Wallace/Mike Bostock
(Winner of the Times Educational Supplement's Junior Information
Book Award and the Kurt Maschler Award)
0-7445-3639-1   £4.99

CATERPILLAR CATERPILLAR
by Vivian French/Charlotte Voake
Shortlisted for the Kurt Maschler Award
0-7445-3636-7   £4.99

A FIELD FULL OF HORSES
by Peter Hansard/Kenneth Lilly
0-7445-3645-6   £4.99

Walker Paperbacks are available from most booksellers, or by post from B.B.C.S., P.O. Box 941, Hull, North Humberside HU1 3YQ

24 hour telephone credit card line 01482 224626

To order, send: Title, author, ISBN number and price for each book ordered, your full name and address,
cheque or postal order payable to BBCS for the total amount and allow the following for postage and packing:
UK and BFPO: £1.00 for the first book, and 50p for each additional book to a maximum of £3.50.
Overseas and Eire: £2.00 for the first book, £1.00 for the second and 50p for each additional book.

Prices and availability are subject to change without notice.